To _THE LEILS_

From _Angie - Ian_

x   x

Other giftbooks by Helen Exley:

Dog Quotations   Kittens!
Glorious Cats   Horse Quotations

Published simultaneously in 1998 by Exley Publications in Great Britain, and
Exley Publications LLC in the USA.
Copyright © Helen Exley 1998
Illustrations © Maria Teresa Meloni 1998
Edited by Helen Exley
The moral right of the author has been asserted.

12 11 10 9 8 7 6 5 4 3 2 1

ISBN 1-86187-021-3

A copy of the CIP data is available from the British Library on request. All rights reserved. No
part of this publication may be reproduced or transmitted in any form or by any means,
electronic or mechanical, including photocopy, recording or any information storage and retrieval
system without permission in writing from the Publisher.

Typeset by Delta, Watford.
Printed in Hungary.

Exley Publications Ltd, 16 Chalk Hill, Watford, Herts WD1 4BN, UK.
Exley Publications LLC, 232 Madison Avenue, Suite 1206, NY 10016, USA.

To Signora Anna Bargellini, my grandmother, for all her help in the making of this book – Maria.

Acknowledgements: A very special thank you to all those who helped supply the "models" for this book,
especially: Lagniappe Labradors, Springfield VA; Brandy Station, Midland VA; S.R.O. Lhasa Apsos,
Reading, PA; M.P.K. Sams, Westminster MD; Siberian Husky, Mary Anne Posch, (301) 797-0993; Apple
Blossom Beagles, Pottstown PA – all USA. The publishers are grateful for permission to reproduce copyright
material. Whilst all efforts have been made to trace copyright holders, we would be pleased to hear from any
not here acknowledged. Celia Haddon: *Faithful to the End*, © 1991 Celia Haddon, published Hodder
Headline Publishing plc. Mary McGrory: from Mary McGrory column; © 1990 Universal Press Syndicate.
Adrian Mitchell: "To My Dog" © Adrian Mitchell. Available in *Balloon Lagoon* (Orchard Books 1997)
reprinted by permission of The Peters Fraser and Dunlop Group Ltd on behalf of Adrian Mitchell.
Educational Health Warning! Adrian Mitchell asks that none of his poems are used in connection with any
examinations whatsoever. Ogden Nash: "Please Pass The Biscuit", published Little, Brown and Co, Inc.
Dorothy Parker: "Toward the Dog Days", from *Here Are Dogs*, © 1931 Dorothy Parker.

PUPPIES!

Edited by Helen Exley

Illustrations by Maria Teresa Meloni

EXLEY

NEW YORK • WATFORD, UK

"PUPPIES FOR SALE"

"Some enchanted evening...."
And so it is with pups and people.
A seething mass of small, yapping, prancing
puppies – and one stands out like a star.
Your puppy.

...

Choose the boldest, the bravest,
the brightest, they say.
But who is the one at the back, all fur and eyes
and desperation?
Willing you to notice her.
Willing you to take her home.

PAM BROWN

❤ *Love* ❤

$\mathcal{A}$ dog has one aim in life. To bestow his heart.

J. R. ACKERLEY

$\mathcal{S}$ign on bulletin board:
Puppies for sale: The only love that money can buy.

$\mathcal{G}$ive a pup a home and a little love
and he will give you his heart forever.

PAM BROWN

I, who had had my heart full for hours, took advantage of an early moment of solitude, to cry in it very bitterly. Suddenly a little hairy head thrust itself from behind my pillow into my face, rubbing its ears and nose against me in a responsive agitation, and drying the tears as they came.

ELIZABETH BARRETT BROWNING

*B*uy a pup and your money will buy love unflinching.

RUDYARD KIPLING

The little one, the wobbly one, the one you
have to carry round,
buttoned into your cardigan – the one that's
going to cost a fortune in vet's bills.
The one who's car sick. The one who panics
every time there's a knock – and would
flatten itself under the bed in silent terror
if there was a burglar.
The one you're going to keep.

CHARLOTTE GRAY

TRUST

We have not to gain his confidence or his friendship: he is born our friend; while his eyes are still closed, already he believes in us: even before his birth, he has given himself to man.

MAURICE MAETERLINCK,
FROM "MY DOG"

A dog will forgive you faster than any human.

PETER GRAY

Pug is come! – come to fill up the void left by false and narrow-hearted friends. I see already that he is without envy, hatred, or malice – that he will betray no secrets, and feel neither pain at my success nor pleasure in my chagrin.

GEORGE ELIOT (MARY ANN EVANS)

A dog believes you are what you think you are.

JANE SWAN,
FROM "DOG QUOTATIONS"

"LOVE ME, PLEASE!"

*T*he average dog has one request to all humankind.
Love me.

HELEN EXLEY

A cat meeting its new owners debates
whether they know how to scratch behind the ears
and if the food is good.
A dog says "I love you. Please, please,
please love me too."

PAMELA DUGDALE

Happiness is a warm puppy.

CHARLES SCHULZ

You come home.
The puppy throws itself at you.
"Where have you been? You've been so
long. I missed you, missed you, missed
you. I love you, love you, love you.
What's in the bag? Something for me?
Oh, let me lick your ear. Oh, let me
chew your gloves. You're HOME!"

PAM BROWN,
FROM "DOG QUOTATIONS"

A dog running for joy of living
is happiness personified.

PETER GRAY

Puddles, chews, wriggles...
LITTLE NUISANCE!

Montmorency's ambition in life is to get in the way and be sworn at. If he can squirm in anywhere where he particularly is not wanted... he feels his day has not been wasted.

JEROME K. JEROME

Any washed dog considers it his bounden duty to get unwashed as soon as possible.

CLARA ORTEGA

Anybody who doesn't know what soap tastes like never washed a dog.

FRANKLIN P. JONES

There is nothing so wet as a wet dog.

JENNY DE VRIES,
FROM "DOG QUOTATIONS"

A door is what a dog is perpetually on the
wrong side of.

OGDEN NASH

However large the house a puppy will always
be underfoot.

PAMELA DUGDALE

The trouble with a very happy puppy
is that it leaks.

CHARLOTTE GRAY

ALL PAWS AND SKIN!

There always seems to be more skin to a
puppy than it can possibly need.

...

A puppy has more paws than he knows
what to do with.

...

Puppies look like very small children
whose mothers have bought a size or two
too big in clothes.
To give them growing room.

MAYA V. PATEL

Innocent, lovable idiots!

One can teach even a tiny dog discipline.
"Go in your basket"
says Master is his sternest voice.
And the puppy obeys.
Enters the basket, tail down,
turns round a time or two
– and then leaps out
beaming from ear to ear
and prances over for a pat
– a virtuous and obedient dog.

...

*E*very pup is convinced there is
something completely delicious
inside a rubber ball.

...

*F*ence in your garden,
block all gaps with wood and wire.
Spread the lawn with toys.
And after a while the man next door will
knock on your door – a jubilant puppy
squirming in his arms.

...

A pup brought up in a loving family believes
that everyone is lovable and that they all
adore very small, bouncy, licky dogs.

PAM BROWN

Silly-Billy!

There is nothing so solemnly silly
as a puppy.

CLARA ORTEGA

There are puppies so dim-witted you
wonder if it's safe to rear them. But they
smile contentedly, and empty their food
dishes, and plod happily behind their siblings
– and are the first to be chosen by
prospective buyers.

PETER GRAY

FAT TUMMIES

One rattle of the biscuit tin and you've got
friends for life.
They sit and stare with solemn eyes, and if you
don't take the hint, you get barked at.

JANINE CHUBB, AGE 10

A puppy can smell dinner
through double glazing
and heavy oaken doors
and brick and concrete
and a casserole dish.

PAMELA DUGDALE

A dog desires affection
more than its dinner.
Well – almost.

CHARLOTTE GRAY

A satiated puppy is a furry skin
stuffed so full it seems in imminent
danger of exploding.
"Tighter than a drum"
is totally inadequate.
Say, rather,
"Tighter than a puppy's tum".

MAYA V. PATEL

A WRIGGLE OF PUPS

What can we call them?...
A huddle of pups?
A wriggle of pups?
A squirm, a shove,
A muddle of pups?
A drowse of pups. A sprawl of pups.
A totally out of this world of pups.
And all gathering the energy
to become a rush, a plunge, a stampede of pups.

CLARA ORTEGA

HUMANS IN TRAINING

A child is given a belief in itself
by the trust in a puppy's eyes.

MARGOT THOMSON

Puppies are nature's remedy for feeling unloved...
plus numerous other ailments of life.

RICHARD ALLAN PALM,
FROM "MARTHA, PRINCESS OF DIAMONDS", 1963

If the doctor insists that you try exercise,
acquire a puppy.
He will take over the entire treatment.

JENNY DE VRIES

To acquire a pet is to take on years of care and companionship – while knowing parting will inevitably come.
And so we learn to live life to the full, to cherish every moment.

...

A puppy, though so small, can teach a child to think itself into another skin –
to see the world through other eyes –
to care for a creature other than itself.

PAM BROWN

"THIS IS THE BOSS!"

Most dog owners are at length able to teach themselves to obey their dog.

ROBERT MORLEY

Daisy, her name is.... It is not the name that I should have selected; she was named that when I got her, on which day she immediately took over the management of my life.

DOROTHY PARKER

LITTLE CLOWN!

A puppy skittering across a polished floor
is pure unadulterated Disney.

PETER GRAY

The dog was created specially for children.
He is the god of frolic.

HENRY WARD BEECHER

Why is it that puppies on leashes always go the
wrong way round a tree?

PAMELA DUGDALE

It's just a matter of getting my legs
to go the same way as one another
all at the same time
and I'll be there....

...

This is the pup that will worry a glove to death.
Kill a shoe.
Rip a toilet roll to shreds
– and run a mile if it sees a mouse.

PAM BROWN

... Foss took this ancient responsibility very seriously. He used to chase aeroplanes, rushing out into the garden and barking at them till they flew away. Then he would come in again, breathing rather heavily, with an expression of satisfaction at a job well done.

CELIA HADDON,
FROM "FAITHFUL TO
THE END"

MINI "JAWS"

Indoors, he developed the habit of sofa-eating; he became, indeed, a veritable addict. Give that dog an ordinary sofa, such as your furniture dealer would be glad to let you have for a nominal sum, and he could make a whole meal off it. If you ran out of sofas, he would be philosophical about the matter – he was always delightfully good-humored – and make a light snack of a chintz-covered arm-chair. Once, I recall, he went a-gypsying and used a set of Dickens, the one with the Cruikshank illustrations, for a picnic lunch.

DOROTHY PARKER,
FROM "TOWARD THE DOG DAYS"

A pup learns very early to bring you your slippers.
What's left of them.

MARGOT THOMSON

The pup that ate cushions, slippers, balls of wool
starts to grow into a calmer, wiser creature.
Who loves you with all its heart.
And brings you gifts.
Half-rotten rabbits.
Fallen branches.
Next door's Sunday roast!

PETER GRAY

Pups fall suddenly asleep

asprawl where they at last keeled over.

They twitch with dreams.

Their paws run through endless meadows

– then one eye opens

and they're off again.

Nirvana must be very like a replete puppy's sleep.
A rapture beyond dreams.

PAM BROWN

HELPLESS AND ALONE...

*L*ittle dogs left outside shops are frantic or
despairing or resigned.
Or simply quietly miserable.
They watch the door.
And turn ecstatic at the sight of Her
– leaping and spinning, nuzzling, kissing,
wagging everything it's possible to wag.
She is half embarrassed by such rapture
– but glad to know that a little pat
will put its world to rights.

MAYA V. PATEL

"**W**on't be long" means nothing to a dog.
All he knows is that you are GONE.

JANE SWAN,
FROM "DOG QUOTATIONS"

Oh, the saddest of sights in a world of sin
Is a little lost pup with his tail tucked in!

ARTHUR GUITERMAN

I ache when I see a lost dog. I am behind his
eyes. I am inside his head. I feel the panic rise.

MARION C. GARRETTY

New owners of small dogs are determined to be
kind, but firm, to establish the proper pecking
order, to instill obedience. To make quite sure
that the puppy knows its place. So there they are.
Food bowl. Basket. Blanket. Pup.
In the kitchen.
Anxious owners snug in bed, door shut – and,
for the puppy's sake, hardening their hearts.
It takes the pup an hour or two – but, with luck,
only half an hour – of sobbing, wailing, howling,
moaning, whimpering, of scrabbling, thumping
and shoving things around.
Before it is curled up on the bed.
Just for tonight.
Or the next fifteen years.

PAM BROWN

THEY FORGIVE US EVERYTHING

Animals are such agreeable friends – they
ask no questions, they pass no criticisms.

GEORGE ELIOT (MARY ANN EVANS),
FROM "GILFIL'S LOVE-STORY"

The great tie that binds us to dogs is not
their fidelity or their charm or
anything else but the fact that they are
not critical of us.

SYDNEY HARRIS

Our dogs will love and admire the meanest of us, and feed our colossal vanity with their uncritical homage.

AGNES REPPLIER

The great pleasure of a dog is that you make a fool of yourself with him and not only will he not scold you, but he will make a fool of himself too.

SAMUEL BUTLER

WHEN LONELINESS HAS GONE

To hold a living creature,
to learn its loveliness,
to feel its heart beat in our hands,
to know its trust, is at last to
understand that we are kin.
Is to rejoice in life.
Is to lose all loneliness.

...

If friends fail us, if the phone is silent
and the postman passes
Our dog will touch our knee, and
smile, and say
Who cares?
All the more time for us to be together.
Come for a walk.
This is a splendid day.

PAM BROWN

A kind of language

Thousands of generations of dogs have, in their heart of hearts, believed that one day, if they listen hard enough, and concentrate, they will eventually master human speech.

MAYA V. PATEL

Most dogs don't think they are human; they know they are.

JANE SWAN

No one appreciates the very special genius of your conversation as a dog does.

CHRISTOPHER MORLEY

A pup does not know words.
It just hears love.
Or anger.
…

To be loved by a cat one must become half cat.
To be loved by a dog one must accept him as
half human.

PAMELA DUGDALE

The dog hesitated for a moment, but presently
made some little advances with his tail. The child
put out his hand and called him. In an apologetic
manner the dog came close, and the two had an
interchange of friendly pattings and waggles.

STEPHEN CRANE,
FROM "A DARK-BROWN DOG"

I marvel that such
Small ribs as these
Can cage such vast
Desire to please.

OGDEN NASH

A dog is the only thing on this
earth that loves you more
than he loves himself.

JOSH BILLINGS
(HENRY WHEELER SHAW)

SERVANTS, GUARDS, FRIENDS

Cat stood at the cave mouth.
"I think I love you," she said.
"I will fit you into my schedule."
Dog stood at the cave mouth.
"I know I love you," she said.
"Take my life, my form, my capabilities
and shape them as you will."

HELEN THOMSON

Dogs, bless them, operate on the premise that human beings are fragile and require incessant applications of affection and reassurance. The random lick of the hand and the furry chin draped over the instep are calculated to let the shaky owner know that a friend is nearby.

MARY MCGRORY

FOR LIFE!

He is very imprudent, a dog is. He never makes
it his business to inquire whether you are
in the right or in the wrong, never bothers as to
whether you are going up or down upon life's
ladder, never asks whether you are rich or poor,
silly or wise, sinner or saint. Come luck or
misfortune, good repute or bad, honour or
shame, he is going to stick to you, to comfort
you, to guard you, and give his life for you....

JEROME K. JEROME

THAT SPECIAL BOND

Intellectuals have sneered at the human-dog friendship and condemned it as "sentimental". Yet, despite their hostile propaganda, the loving bond between our two species persists. Neither tyrants nor bureaucrats nor intellectual snobs can abolish this love, thank goodness.

CELIA HADDON,
FROM "FAITHFUL TO THE END"

*A dog is a chance to express
yourself without the fear of
seeming foolish, a chance to
share emotions that others of
our kind too often repel —
tenderness, outright joy, love.*

GAIL PETERSEN,
FROM "A BOOK OF FRIENDSHIP"

This gentle beast
This golden beast
laid her long chin
along my wrist

and my wrist
is branded
with her love
and trust

and the salt of my cheek
is hers to lick
so long as I
or she shall last

ADRIAN MITCHELL

All right, so I don't know how to use a
litter tray or to bury my garden messes.
And I can only go out of the yard on a leash.
And I bark at everything.
And I'm not very good at washing myself.
And I roll in doubtful substances.
And I cock my leg up other people's cars.
And I smell a bit iffy in warm weather.
But I love you, love you, love you,
and I will go on loving you till the day I die....

PAM BROWN